DO YOU WANT TO KNOW HOW DOES IT FEEL LIKE?

A GARDEN WHICH HAS NO FLOWERS JUST LEAVES AND STEMS.

ANJALI UPADHYAY

This book is dedicated to my most beautiful parents, i can write many chapters about.

This book is dedicated to my mom, who wants be to be perfect. I just try to complete my work on time. Also Mom because she let's me buy makeup though I have no where to go. lol because she really nice.

To my dad, who told me that rejection is a good thing atleast you got it when my first ever book got rejected which i wrote with my own efforts and hardwork and for your shoes are the one I would really want to put on.

To everyone who supported me to write and appreciate my work.

My brother Apoorv who helped me cope up depression.

My relatives for good criticism.

And a hypothetical member of my family, my dog.

I was joking I am not mad.

To my readers too because they are the who read and actually understands me and for spending their precious time.

To almighty God for giving me so many things in my life.

I hope the title "Do you want to know how does it feels like" work.

Contents

Acknowledgements   *vii*

Prologue   *ix*

1. Meeting An Old Friend Of Mine   1

2. Everyone Is In The Room   10

3. You Wish It Was Me   14

4. It's You   21

5. We Did It To Ourselves   25

6. Sorry It Had To Come To This.   32

7. Its Been A Long Time Since We Fell In Love.   39

8. Push The Limits Of Love   45

9. After Party   47

10. They Didn't Make Things Worth I'll Spend My   48
    Money To.

11. The Fort We Live In   51

Epilogue   53

Acknowledgements

Some scenes are reference to other novel, movies or webshow like twilight breaking dawn 1.

Just to complete the word limit.

Prologue

It was dark night, shivering cold. I wrote a poem sitting on my poem as it says:

"*Many days have passed, Suppressed my emotions,*
Should I feel compassionate about my self
Or is it too bad.
Would it show a sign of recovery?
Peace in sadness is my new bakery.
I can relate to a daughter whose mother died
I cried, dried leaves stuck in my intestine
You feel like that pain too when we cry?
For there is nothing left to pause and take a breath,
I feel the cold hit my chest and head.
I take support and roll my eyes to you again
What if you woke and hugged for you are not dead.
But it was better heard you will never come back,
The sun melted the snow stuck to my body,
My jammed foot now work like engine body,
The sun was you, snow my pain,
Make me heal, tan by tan.
I am going darker than you think,
Sweats making me lighter as i shrink,
My wounds have burned, the poison won't spread,
You to bite me back, all healthy and well.
- Anjali Upadhyay"

Some random song was playing behind as I entered the hallway.

Wine ka bohot bada fountain tha. Abh toh common hogaya hai sheher mein. Bohot bada potrait that dulha dulhan ka tha. Bhul jaun kya mein uss din ko?

Ekdum bahr se foreingn queens ke fort jaisa mahal tha jahan mein aachi khasi badi fully embroidered gown pehenke gyi thi. Ni pata tha itta kya khas hoga ki ek puri book likh duingi issi sab ke baare mein.

This novel is about Shnaya, a girl. I'll tell her prologue. I am new at writing, so with practice I'll gain a hand on this. Just this one prologue and I'll be able to crack it. Hope you guys are considerate. If you want to not see me struggle through expressing emotions (though girls are good at expressing feelings but its difficult for me) which initially I will, skip the first part, you can skip this prologue. Girls are good at expressing feelings. First at time when she is talking to other and the topic should be either a boy or beauty. Second to be honest with the feeling to the whole world is bit challenging. I may bore you intiall and get off the topic. I will try not to and next won't let you skip any chapter I promise. My plan is I want to give you a story initially. Why?

Because

Do you get this feeling too. When you start to reading a novel and you don't know what the story is and we read the first lines in hurry or restlessness or with utter curiosity after seeing the title. So I don't want you to witness this, trust me I wont kill the suspense I'll give you story initially which was supposed to be second last chapter of the novel. But before, I wanted to talk to you first. I can not ask you your interests, now right here to talk to you but you can listen to a story.

About this book this story is narrated by shnaya the main charater herself. Oh! sorry you read the description already. Thats the reasons those who want to go to the the novel here is brief of prologue. The whole novel is naration by Shnaya, from now. The scene is Shnaya wrote an an autobiography which became a bestseller like every author wants his/her novel to be and she moves to the movie state. Somewhere most of the industry is situated and after gaining this huge success what happens to her life is what she explains in the story.

Beleive me it's not that boring.

After gaining so much fame and after children, should she should be felling blessed about her carrer or should she still run to prove herself every step. She can do both. Settle down and keep working at the same pace or take the different obstacles that comes into her life. The novel is about the correct balance of works by her decisions.Not a schedule of work and vacation. (I can give you one though take a vacation in every 3 months.) Everyone choses to prove themselves this was easy though but sometimes if take a moment and look back we see who are we working so hard for. For a vaction with our family in a nice resort (or we are working for ourselves to just live), so that future generation can survive and have and to bring all the luxury to our heirloom. They can earn on their own too. But we care for who are ours.

Just a random thought came what will happen if someday each one of us got everything present on the world, sooner or later. Then we would work for its maintance and food to survive because it has to be fresh or new. Or let's take a difference in the situtation. We got huge houses enough sufficient clothes are bought already from our ancestors, we have no one to give it to. Everyone has there own and too many. The top brands are long gone. There was nothing left to be made. Girls wore boys clothes and boys wore girls too. We have started it now only. No not the end of imagination for more clothes but everyone had too many, (this was for sarcasm.) Similarly shops of tiles and everything will end someday. Everything would initially depend on necessity, then luxury and the again necessity maybe. Actually if machines came for croping then enternaiment would work that too free why would they need money. If you think transportation Sustainable environment is coming into role so every thing will work on battery and batteries can be charged by solar. One day it will come when things would be this good as we are saving money like hell. Our parents have forgotten to spend money on them selves. My moms's shoping is my gift. There would be no problem in this world as people would just admire actors and would try to become like one. There would be no dowry for marrige and no robbery. Maybe the boders will dissolve what would we fight for. For entertainment purpose we'll work. Money won't be a boundary to love and so won't be a reason to skip friends b'day plans.

I wrote about this global issue I should have just sent it to Ambani's I know I am sorry. I don't have there number. This is a love novel. things about love should be here but sorry I told you I am new it didn't wasted your time though I gave you an insight of future.

Let's start like novel supposed to, every thing is said by shnaya from here.

"Thankyou again for coming. Enjoy."

I said as I came down the stairs. Everyone went to eat in the very extra buffet. I mean I was just mumbling who creates so big uttensils. There was a wine fountain too. By looking at that I just told my self everything is developing.

There were different types of ballons in loops and all was planned by event manger. Children were fighting with their parents to dance and danced on all wrong songs they were supposed to, they didn't understood anything, it was dj's mistake. But parents enjoyed the song.After becoming a parent there's no time to listen to songs. I don't believe in dialogue, Yes I don't relate to you. So let this story be in a gossip way.

I have this this huge family of my mom sides who celebrates every month. For coming from a childhood where only mom dad were everything, physically the whole world. It's a bit too much to have guest around. Today was our little kiki's 5th birthday. She is growing fast I was asked to say something on this occasion something lovely about her future and proud parents, not just me but with my cousin sister I have to do this.. We came to this big hotel just for the relative's they have planned it for. I was asked to design a 6 feet potrait too of kavya which after party my sister took home along with ballons for she said kavya will enjoy the decorated home too and the hotel people would anyway throw it. I like my sister a lot whose child kavya is.

Lets skip the speech for now and meet people in the party.

So guest one my (mausis) aunts who are the critics of my family but they love me a lot and we all have people looking for our flaws for our good.

"Today I had a conversation with my watchmen" says one of my aunt "You know we have 6 street dogs in our parking lot of my apartment its such a trouble to carry food from there, even when we leave they come to smell, its so unhygienic. I told Wasim (watchmen)to do something. He was so chilled he said out of them four are from our colony others are outsiders. Two of them are bitch who will leave today, I've given them some medicine." there was a sense of ownership in Wasim as he owns the world. he said to my aunt not to care about it. I get all this information by her looks when she narrats it. She is good at mimicry. At last she leaves and say I have no hope in Wasim.

Then came the most important guests we have my sisters inlaws. Her father was so pleased to have them.

Her father in law to my dad " You have literally vanished after the wedding"

My father has a jolly nature he has great personality to be friends with any one. Once we went to a road trip to Shimla where we took a bus to travel my father told his biography to the conductor, the conductor told his biography to they talked a lot and my father says everyone story is intresting irrespective of money they have afterall god has written it.

So after the shimla we went to himachal where as we were touring the nearby places too. Their we again met the condutors he shook hands with my dad and was very happy to have us. He didn't took the money too. So getting back to the scene.

My dad replied with a smile and they had their own conversation.

By the time I am friends with my sister's brother in law I said to him "we know magic how we managed to so called 'vanish'"

He with much more sarcasm said "magic or blackmagic"

I said "I agree you're smart"

"I am smater than you think girl."

"Mmm.. I think you are what you are. I think you are decent smart like how kendall said cute jeans."

"I will reply about myself about what you just said later but listening to kendal jenner and all from your mouth you are going towards becoming a girl who will not put hair behind or wrap it how it should be when it comes in front of eyes or disturbing you, rather you would put it on side of your face, cleaning the flick which hardly makes difference. And start to saying things with a pause. Actually with the extras.. emotions and feeling of things which are already mutual"

"Believe me. I was about to say I love their accent and their clothes. I gonna buy whole damn skims.." Before he could complete and I went on continued

"Oh!"and he smiled at me like a dad would looking at his daughter while she is playing

I knew he wasn't interested in the conversation. So i went to points he talked about. Advice do it to get attention,

"You said about the mutuals. Belive me mutuals feeling are most attractive. Relating to someone is what we look for."

"Are you looking looking for someone relatable?" he teased me

He then says " So hows your friend?when are you both getting married." sarcastically. Actually this was my question I used to ask him. I belived in love marriages. and he in arranged. He says he can nail a marriage by just family help and relation. We enjoy spending time together with family and that is what happiness is supposed to be in the family. Caring for parent and children. But I think no. Love for eachother is what family is. When some something presious you feel about yourself. When we start to enjoy luxury and not just respect it and keep it is what family is.We did a bet.

He said "I'll marry a girl of my parent's choice and if you get a boy of your dreams you marry him. Let's see whose marriage is more successful." and he is supposed to get married at this age. Let's get back to the scene.

"So what's wrong in that you are supposed to have children in this age Go ahead and.. go propose that girl in red.."

"No she is a bit too goddy."

"Hehe.. Are you really choosing? We are not supposed to put girls in category."

"No I didn't intended to. Your brain did it automatically. She fell on her own. By the a theory says 90% of people are judged by their apperance. It's automatic."

"Meine to hardly shoping kari hai. sab didi ke kapde hain. Btw which category do I belong to my didi ke dewar." I said with extra possesivness, keeping hand on his shoulder and pointing his chest and then started to laugh.

"Abh bata diya hai to bhabhi jaisi he lagti ho"

"You mean bhabhi category. huh?.. mmm.. the most searched porn word" I said with litterally laughter.

"Mera woh matlab bilkul ni tha. "he bursted out laughing.

Meanwhile my mom came to me she was wearing pink banarasi saree with red lipstick and the boy I was talking to was named Minnie it was his nickname. He is an engineer and I have dated his brother Annie.

"Kya baate hori thi aap dono ke beech mein.. aur Shnaya thoda dheere to hasa karo, sab hasni naam rakh deinge." it was a sarcastic and over concious behaviour she has lived or that generation was making people perfect. I don't know.

while she drank the soup which was served by waiter.

"Shaadi ka bolri thi mein.. inko wo red ladki dekhai meine"

"Chup kuch bhi bolti ho"he said

"Aree wo ni brigadeir ki beti hai woh... ladki to apni samany parivar se karna chaiheye. Aap he dono kyu ni karlete shaadi itte aache se to abhi baat karre the. Mera aur aapke mummy papa ka bhi kaam bhi asaan ho jaiyega"

"Aree kaha aap bhi "i said

"Mere liye toh behen jaisi hai" he said as he actually knew that at a certain time I was very much close to his brother.

"Ye mere high attraction ka consquence hai."I replied

"Samjha ni.. btw I am not attracted to you"

" I didn't mean you but abh boldiye ho Toh itta has ke baat kyu karre ho"

"For the first time a girl is being creepy."

"I was pretending to be creep. You can laugh with me.."

Before I could complete that line. He said

"Hasna itta zaroori ni hai tumhe creep banna pade"

"Oh please.. tumhe uncomfortable laga issiliye bolre ho."I turned the conversation back to fun.

I laughed.

Then my mom was busy meeting guest as a I saw my ex, I hate to take his name too

"Aacha lagra h aap se milke, ruko mein aapne bete ko bulari"his mom to my mom.

As her soon as he came he side ways hugged me, as soon as he tried to do so I pushed him back. I made an excuse

"Thoda sa claustrophobia sa hai. Abhi lift mein thi na."

I actually didn't wanted to hug him, get any closer or even look at him. Why do he even hug me? He should take it as a compliment I am not hitting him. Why does he want to pretend nothing happenned? He can skip me but as I know he is a liar. We have moved foreword in our lives . Any one would in 3years. It never mattered to him I am in the function present too or maybe it has become easy for him to attend the family function where I am. Doesn't he get reminded of all the good memory we had together. It' a different feeling when you look at a person in the party you have history about.

"Tum.. woh naam kya tha ladke ka jiski photo tumne dikhayi thi Annie.. oh haa Abhimanyu. Dost hai tumhara?Friend."

"Nahi to aunti mera koi friend Abhimanyu ni hai.(Though I have him)"

"Aree dekho isse jo photo humne dekhi" his mom to him

"haan.. mereko account bhi dekha dena kisse milli tumhe cause mera aaccount to private hai."

He then understood he was syncing my photo and so they changed the topic of discussion. It didn't bother to me, him checking my social media. When he is the topic I am most conifident now about my decision towards him. But when I am alone and moments we shared together reminds it really hurts hard. When he is right in front of me and looks straight into my eyes, things melt down a bit. But Ignoring helps. Ignoring is not bad. Like how we sometimes ignore the creeps, national issues, work at family time.

I then asked myself who is Abhimanyu to me. A close friend. No.

So before you know my reply this story is about him. Lets know him and later conversation is boring.

Not to kill you with suspense he is someone who will take care of my parents too.

Meri didi ke party me kuch unke friends bhi aaye the bohot party karte hai meri ko kisi mein bhi invite ni kare..

1

Meeting an old friend of mine

So my ex- boyfriend used me and I was shattered. I was unwell for 90 day. Every moment seemed year. My parents couldn't handle me. Eventually I ended up to psycologist. I thought this is end of my world. My first cry started when he said "I cannot bear you anymore." We never fought in our 6month relationship, maybe it wasn't true thats why or he was IITian 'the very husband' I actually cared maybe less about.

Pehle mein khud ke sath khush thi phir usse dekha jana wo bhi kitna relatable hai itna he khush. Uski khushi mein khushi dhundhli but 6 mahine baad jisme promise humne roz baat kari hai wo khushi jo humari thi suddenly end hogayi.

May he be happy with who ever he meets, at last. The story of him and I is so boring I had to put some spices to get it to you but at the end of the day its sad so lets skip it. I started with him because he is this crucial in my story.

A year or two later I joined instagram where I met this boy who is muffin to my story. He is damn gorgeous.The first time I saw his profile my eyes started shining. I love the cuteness of his face. He is dropdead georgeous. He had a girlfriend she's older than us. They are perfect couple as supposed to be says, she was as intelligent as him, smart and way too arogant to me. Not as beautiful as I am which is rude to say but let me believe it. I used to tease her she had shinchan voice. She is nice to everyone in general. She'll get someone else.

Crushes hote kyu hain love stories banti kyu hain I wonder. Log khushi dhund lete he hain kahin na kahin par humpe depend karta surity khush hone ki. Abh hum chod toh nahi sakte, supposed to be married to that guy, suppose to respect his parents. Kitne answers yaad rakheinge? Aapne andar se aana chaiye na ki chalo shaadi karlete hain, thankfullness honi chaiye uske maa baap ke liye itna ki karz hai kyuki kamse kam 50 saal to humare sath he jiyega na.

Lets me introduce you to Abhimanyu he used to study with me. He is an IITian too, IIT bombay. Thankgod not from computer science branch. The first time I saw him I was like he is out of my league. He didn't need any frame to his glasses. He is focused always. He got htis beautiful eyes deep black and his skin shines in sun (Everyone's does but his is special. Just joking).

I am at Chicago LA and so is he. I recently bought a house here with wooden floor. Thank you for the wishes. I am going to him today. I am damn nervous. Oh he is the muffin guy. I can't express my feelings though girls are good at it because I can't stop smiling when the topic is him. I didn't elaborated his beauty to me too and how much he meant to me.

So the scenario is I'll say I have no Indian friends (Secretly I many of them and they are very pretty. One of them is acquaintance to me from my childhood) and I am nervous to do that. How can I be I wonder. Its his girlfriend or so called "close friend" that makes me furios.

Do minute ko toh aisa lagra tha kisi ka basabasaya ghar thodne jaari par wo ladki smart hai use koi aur mil jayega aur abh milke bichadna toh dastur hai.

It is lunch time 12 o'clock. I could have taken with me some fancy gift flowers which I also gifted my ex (I wonder what he did with my flower after the breakup. I didn't wanted myself to remind of him and flower would every moment at his door too) or some toy for this engineer guy (But love isn't a toy and I totally do) but I don't want him remember me some girl who is just caring and put me in the mom category. I want any day when we have our last hug together (I had my heart broken already so when I used to be alone I craved for his hug so this time i decided i would really ask him for a last hug), my last request it is he want him to be not hated by me, to be remembered in his best behavior.

I walked into his office. My first feeling was 'Should I wash my face again?'. I felt dirty. The floor was this white that I wanted to remove my sandals before I enter. He had his Glass door cabin where I saw him after years. We went to same coaching in my 9th. He was working I was stuck I took fruits with me for him.

Wo dur tha but meri ankhon ke andar tha mere dil ke andar mere andar. Wo literally bas gaya tha meri ankhon mein.

He came out and noticed me. He came to me and said to me "hi you are Shnaya, right? We used to go to the same coaching. Do you remember me?"

"Yes Of course I do." I replied

"Nice" He must be busy so he got distracted with his work. "The reception is to the right. Help yourself. By the way I have my lunch in 2 minutes. If you can make it we can talk... I am new to this city."

"Why not, I am here for you."I said in a sarcastic tone. He smiled and went to his main office.

I went to reception.

"May I know where the wash basin is?"

"It's to the left. Let me take you" said the receptionist. She headed me to the wash basin where I washed my fruits which I bought on the way before eating rather gifting them.

"These covid days we have to be hygienic" I said to the lady there. She was considerate. She gave me look of understanding. I took his picture work subconsciously which turned out to be great. Thanks to my new phone.

I entered his cabin. I said "so you are done with your work. You are anyway topper you can do it later too."

"Just give me five more minute."

I pulled his hand to take him while he was waiting standing for some print. He slipped slightly and we had come literally the closest. He took support from desk but mutually we realized if he took a step forward to balance his twisted feet we would have kissed. Of course we don't want it to happen. So he held my waist with his other hand turned me round himself, pushed me a bit back with a sense of making sure my comfort. Then he stabilized his twisted feet. As soon as this was over the print came out. I handed him the page. He said " Thankyou and sorry for this awkwardness."

I said "I guess the lunch is over. I must leave."

He was relaxed and went back to work. He maybe got confused by my behavior.

"Com'on, don't leave this abrupt. It was not my fault. I'll feel guilty."He said

I said "okay" and sat.

"I have actually come here for you. Before I forget I got some fruits for you"

"Thankyou. So why me?"

"I was just bored I logged into the Instagram saw you are here so why not meet in the same town"

"I thought you were shocked in the hall way seeing me. anyway, its good you have come."

There was awkward silence but not for me my eyes were shinning seeing him.

"you look good with tanya "

"What did you just meant?" he said with a laugh

"I mean com'on I know about you two"

"No there's nothing. We are just friends. There is nothing like what you think. "

"Maybe"

Like that our conversation continued for months in instagram and facebook even at SMS. We continued to text each other we even once talked at the same time at two different social media platform about two different topics. We sent each other memes, got to know taste of each other. I think he miss his school and college alot. He used to like and share meme of that particular category.

Our conversation was not that boring always for instance there was this one incident he told one day her aunt went to pee in bushes where all dogs came of nearby smelling her pee and were staring at her literally, she had to go off. Lol

He also did sometimes flirt in middle too like he once asked me "where's your favorite place to go?"

I said "in Chicago or like whole world"

"Stop there only I was just asking some place nearby to go to not a honeymoon vacation"

From initial conversation to flirt and this friendly environment was a long run.

But humne kisi tarah tay kar he liya aur kar liya tha to chalna to tha he aur wo rasta hum chaleinge nange pair chaleinge, rait pe chaleinge, dhup pe chaleinge. Toll tax pe toll bhi denge chalte chalte.. lol just kidding waise chalne walo ka tax ni lagta.

The lines I heard coming from a topper guy was way too amusing. He numbered his family members. One was his mom his #1 his top most priority. He told me. He was moving out of his comfort zone. We became friends too soon and I entered the club of his close friends. We posted pictures everyday of sky and of each other.

We went on a coffee date where I made his potrait which was the first time he kissed my forehead sideways from back. I didn't felt anything for days. It felt like a die heart fan got to meet his celebrity.

He wrote an original song which he sang in a club with it sounded like gulzar

before going he said to me if the audience thew tomatoes, be ready to run. but I said I beleive in you. I insisted him to go alot. He was this nevous, he had shakky hands. He came back from the stage twicewithout singing. I motivated him. Said it's really few people even if it didn't make it which I know you will it hardly matters, no one knows you. And the probability of you being shamed is zero in your mathematics terms.

"Okay don't record it please"

"Everyone is recording but"

"They don't know me"

"I already had many special moments my parents are proud of, the academics one"

"Are but for the shaadi ka rishta, we have to send some thing to represent the entertainment category"

"I'll marry you I didn't got any girl" he now understand my joke and when its time time for me to laugh at it he says something else funny to distract my hard worked joke.

"i am joking" he continued

"So did I... go now'

So last he went with confidence and The lyrics said something:

Com'on and now hold my hand, baby we'll die right end
Slowly we'll fall apart maybe this is how its meant.
But before we go through, I want to tell you
The snow was not much as my height, yes I stood here all night.
Still as you left, pressed my eyes to hold tears and breathe.
Com'om say it the only person i'll giveup my heater is you.
Cause anyway it feels cold without you.

...

The song continued.. it had more such preety lines. I loved it and so did everyone. He even promised me to write a hindi song about me.

We started to know each other pretty well. And I was not born yesterday I can feel a connection too we shared.

One day I commented on his picture and that comment was liked by his friends. They were teasing him. I took it as a complement as I am capable to be discussed. I even made a potrait of him in a suit. Actually that broken part of my ex comes in flow sometime. However spending time eventually leads to attachment and me and my ex used to talk for hours. We had age difference of 4 years(annie and I). So his friends used to laugh and say that you are dating a kid and he never fought to them it was I who researched and found Sharukh khan and his wife too had 4 years age difference. Anyway now it seems in such a way. Maybe it's a harsh reality. At that time it seemed as though they were just having fun but our impressssion is something our parterner need to care about. If wouldnt have broken up this novel would have been about us and not Abhimanyu and I.

Abhimanyu se milne ke baad chain ki nend aane lagi pata ni kyu ya shayad itta pyaar karti hoon ki janna he nahi chahti.

Abhimanyu so I belived girlfriend got married she did an arrange marriage. Abhimanyu went to the marriage to help with work. I was not invited he asked me to come along but it was weird to go to a friend you know and you are not invited to.

One day my mom called me

"hi mom " in sleepy tone i said

"Hi! what the hi! My blood pressure is high.You don't get such simple things, at 11 you must be talking to me, its 11:10 now. Have you eaten something?"

"Yes"

"When?"

"At 3:30"

" Its way too late. If you were here, everything would have been proper"

" I had a long day mom at my work." I said as i even went to send the resignation to the office.

" I understand the work but only do you have long day. Your boss is behind you. I am calling your HR and complaining . Its too much "

"He is making everyone of us. Why are you behind everything. So many questions you ask. "

"Why wouldn't I ask? I am your mother. Kept you in my stomach for 9 months. It's my right to ask."

"Now let me ask. Have you eaten your medicines on time?, you checked your blood pressure today?.. Exactly we are on the same page. "

"Leave you have to come.. remember?"

It was summer I have to go back to my own country. I can't skip it. I even have to get my visa extended. If it was in my hand I would have remained here forever. I said bye to Abhimanyu, gave him some flowers.

"Jana hai abh(I have to go)" I said to him just like any ordinary day in his office.

"My office will miss you" he said while putting on his coat.

"My advice would be zyada dil mat lagao. (Don't get attached to me) "

He kissed my forehead and said "Bye, take care" and left for his meeting.

"Agar flight mien mar gyi toh bhul mat jana(don't you dare to forget me if I die today)." I said with a smile.

He had tears when I left. I know he is silly but he is this cute to a friend and fell in love with this child.

2

Everyone is in the room

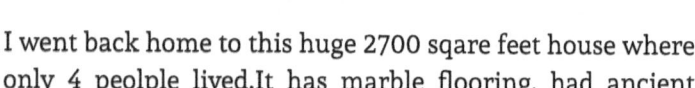

I went back home to this huge 2700 sqare feet house where only 4 peolple lived.It has marble flooring, had ancient design and paintings.

"It's so good to have you here, my child" said my mom kissing my forehead which I wiped. "You know what we are thinking to build a pool for you in your room. We will manage some space there. We'll move a wardrobe and keep it in gallery. You must shift here."

"This was so obvious mom. Have you ever done something for my happiness irrespective of some work behind it?"

"We care for you my child. you don't think the way we do we are your parents if we wouldn't think who would. You have no work there. Our money invested in the house there is such a waste."

"This was the first I asked for your help mom and I am not wasting time there I am studying for my mppsc exam."

"Eventually you have to land up here so why not now"

"I want space and years later that house will have higher rates"

"I don't want to argue anymore. Have you eaten something?"

"You shouldn't I have come from a long way."

"Should I cook something?" said my mom ignoring me.

I fight rather argue with her a lot. She is nice but in money matters not my forte. She loves my brother. He is super rich. I don't know what he does and where is he. I don't care about it too.

Door the knocked and entered my aunt who just keep buying kurtas with plazzos. She is the richest sister of my mom. She is divorced because her husband had an affair.She has a very pretty daughter who's clinic is about to open in a month. My aunt wants me to marry someone as soon as possible and she have list of boys for me.

One of them is whom I am going to meet this weekend. He is my sister's brother in law. They are general middle class people. I am going to take my friend Shruti with me. She is entrepreneur and I know her since class 2. I love her a lot. She has an amazing pet name copper.

I called Shruti.

"Hi. I am in town. Where are you? "

"Hyyy bro. I was anyway thinking of a reunion."

"Before the main point, how is France"

"There is so much freedom. I hooked up with this amazing boy on my last week there."

"Seems interesting, find someone for me too."I replied with a laugh.

"By the way Karan is in town. Do you want to meet him?"

Oh! I forgot to mention she has this super hot brother everyone's mad about. He has such a friendly nature and he parties a lot also has international drugs connection.

"No why would I want to... Anyway I have an official date this Sunday. Please come. My parents set us up. "

"Sure babe. See you there we'll talk about the reunion then only."

"Before I cut the call. Do you have any gossip?"

"Yes I do have one."

"Com'on tell me"

"I can tell you but..."

" why can't you say it? Com'on tell me "

" Later on dude.."

Now I guess she wanted me to beg for the gossip but I tried the reverse psycology.

"Okay let it be."

" Why let it be, it is a verified gossip, like a blue tick one."

"No why bother you"

"I was joking. Are you taking it wrong"

I started smilling and general girl's talk started.

So a week later we went. I got no content to write from him. So let's skip it. He was self obsessed. Much a girly and too particular. I rejected him. He was an MBA. He did ask me a question

"Would you be invested to your aim of your life and leave every thing fun or you would enjoy your life which is worth and we can now ?"

I replied if you love your aim you would leave everything and find happiness and fun in that only.

That day on my instagram something weird happen I got a request from those group we all have of rich bullies, a follow request came from a guy named ajit jain. He was friends with Karan and spoiled as expected. The dark character in any movie with all black outfit to look cool.

People who spend money like water and say it's for happiness.

I was shocked why would he send me request?

About my ex how is he crucial to my story is he made me feel cry. He is not a bad person. Sorry if I potraied him wrong. He was genuenly I nice person i fell in love with.

3

You wish it was me

My friend Shruti called me.

"Hey! Let's have a reunion as I have mentioned before."

"Sure"

"I have talked to Shreya and many other classmates we have. They all agreed and you are last one I am calling to inform as you already know we are going goa next week, will meet at taj there."

"Goa, we are coming!"

Later that day I opened my Instagram, saw Ajit putting some insta stories with air tickets of goa. I called Shreya again.

"Hey sorry to disturb you."

"It's okay, say it"

"You told me once Karan tells you everything. Do you know his friend Ajit?"

"Yes, I know him personally too. He is like brother to me."

"He sent me a follow request on instagram. I wonder why?"

"Did he? He is really conservative. He is there in the trip too; he is coming with my brother."

"I didn't know that you are taking your family with you."

"Lol just my brother is coming to drop me. We'll separate from airport. I hate to travel alone."

"Oh! You can ask them to join us, it'll be fun meeting new people"

"I'll try."

So Ajit is supposed to be hot. He has a mercedes so anyone in it would look god. He is rich so he must be spending money on his maintenance and he liked my photo that one with Abhimanyu. I got surprised. He then posted a photo of a pamphlet of advertisement of farmhouse. My mom was recently interested in buying some farmhouse for my cousin's wedding. Don't worry, not to gift them, we are not that rich. The guest from outstation can stay there plus some small functions can take place the of the wedding. All my cousins are of my same age group, so beneficial for all also no one has a farmhouse in our close family. So we never been to a farmhouse farm house together. I called the number fixed a date after my return from goa to site visit.

So, I went to this goa trip.

Day 1: I was at the reception at taj when they entered. Shruti, Karan and Ajit. They were too happy for I don't know what was the reason. Ajit came near me put his hand inside my hair towards back. His chest was minimalistic to my face. It was way too close. He went like as I thought he is touching my cheeks. I was stuck, paused and was observant for a moment. He then entangled a rose in my hair which he took from back and started laughing with Karan and Shruti.

I got confused by his behavior rather annoyed for my hair. Took that rose out in the direction he putted inn in. He gave an understanding look.

I said "I didn't get what you are doing but it went wrong I guess."

"I was just greeting you (padharo mare desh)" Ajit replied. "By the way, we saw you from the stairs, there is no more room left in the hotel. So, I'll leave you can take mine. Though Taj is where literally everyone wants to stay but I understand you have your friends here. Karan and Shruti are also staying together. We would have done booking earlier."

"It's okay we can share."

He got surprised and started to laugh. He said "Abh mere sath sote hue aachi thodina lagogi (Do you want to sleep with me?)"

"I can sleep with shruti and karan can with you "

Everyone became happy and they felt a sense of intelligence in me.

"So you are coming to my room?" ajit said.

"yes instead of shifting i can keep my luggage at ajit"

"okay follow me."

On entering his room I put my bag in he helped me. I said "Thankyou". We were alone

" I can sleep at the sofa. I want to know you. I wish we can spend more time together. Don't tell karan about this. He is protective towards his sister and her friends."

He spoke so soft, the last line was mumbled.

"So you better be careful" I said sarcasticly

Then my phone rang, it was Abhimanyu's video call. Turned back and picked up the call.

"Flight land hone par call ni kiya. Bhul gyi?(You didn't call on landing)"

"Oh! yes I am sorry. Were you waiting? Aww..."

By the time I could complete my reply Ajit pulled me back hugged me. Rested his face on my shoulder, held my waist and pressed it. He said on microphone "look I am giving massage to your girlfriend" and while saying this he started laughing.

I said " What the fuck, behave" and went out pushing him away. He did a surrender action and said "totally ma'am"

"Sorry Abhi that was annoying he is just a friend."

"Now I got you were busy that why you forgot to call."

"What went wrong with you now."

"Nothing enjoy. I have some work, got to go"

He hung up but I noticed one thing before that call ended he had tears in his eye. He is such a fair hearted child I love. Once told me (Abhimanyu) that when he was in school he used change the pen to write because his crush uses a different pen. He is this cute.

I went back to the room.

"Are you fine? I was just joking and was about to say it but you got offended. I thought you'll introduce me."

"He is not like us. You should have asked me first. He has a soft heart."

"Give me your phone I'll talk to him"

"No thankyou"

I moved the bedsheet and sat on the bed. Ajit came sat next to me.

"What?" I asked

"Nothing just sorry"

"It's fine"

"So did you enjoyed it, me on your waist." he laughed

"Com'on" with a hit from pillow in an annoyed tone.

"Also I'm not dating him."

"Hmm tum toh meri wife ho" he said with a laugh

"Haan ha Future wife" I beated him again and said in much more sarcastic tone.

We became friends in this tour, I made sure he didn't do any ciggrate or drugs. Alcohol is fine. Highest tax goes in it. I started trusting him like a brother in this tour. We actually came the closet on the day 2 where he asked me to dance. We went to a club and he started treating me as his girlfriend but eventually stopped the too much when shreya asked "Is there something between you guys"

We said simultaneously"No"

He is good at changing topic when it came about us.

Emotionally I came close to him as he treated me like his roomate. When ever we were free he used to come to me, put his hand on me and side hug me, like a little sister he wished to have.

I was just being understanding and someone who is super nice approches you, you wouldn't refuse and in the modern world we live in somtimes my heart dissolves bounday in name of decency. There was this picture of us I remember which he uploaded on instagram then was me kissing a puppy and he made a pout towards me. It was a selfie, he took.That time he even teased me

"Should I write happy family there as a caption. Dogs must only live in this world."

"Who will cook for them then if humans die and I really don't want them to hunt each other to survive plus we have some boys like dogs. You for example." I laughed

"Too smart you think you are"

Then came the last night in goa. For the update on Abhimanyu we didn't talked since that day.

"itte dinno se sofe pe sone se peeth akad gyi hai. mein bhi bed use karluin. i mean wahin soo luin."

"kyu nahi" I replied

"aapna no. to dedo"

"kyu"

"abh 3-4 saal baad aapne pati aur baachon ki photo instagram pe kaise dalogi agar mujhe aapna no. ni dogi toh" he teased me again.

"mein ni chahti yaha se jaane ke baad aapn mille, mein chicago jaari hoon"

"chalo mein bhi chal sakta hoon.. dad mere over seas business expand karne ka sochre the."

"nhi mein ni chahti tum peeche aao"

"aise kyu baat kar rahi ho mujhe rona aajayega seriously "

"tum serious bhi hote ho!? chalo sona hai mujhe nend aari hai."

We turned off the lights then few moments later he kept his hand on me I turned to him in a caring expression moved my hand on his head, touched his hair. He opened his eyes and tears fell down.

" Is there anything we can talk about!?I never left my drugs for anyone before."

"Yes there is this one topic I am going to buy a farm from your dad's framhouse. Any suggestion?"

"There is a six thousand square feet farm available.It's of 25 lacs. That's the smallest"

"Why do you think I'll buy the small one"

"Generally old people buy farms you're young."

"Before I get into the actual topic I wanted to talk about something else so this was it."

"I have never been friends to a girl before, I treated you like any of my friend I would. I don't know when I got attached to you. Do you love or even respect me?"

"What is bad about you?Nothing. To get it right, I am not good enough for you." I knew in my head my parents were not as rich as his were.

"What are you talking about?"

"Nothing just beleive me I mean it."

"I'll love every version of you. Every thing I've done since the day I laid eyes on you it was for you. Guess I am an idiot."

"You're not."

"I saw you are together, you are optimised, you are so much smarter than me."

"But I love someone else I didn't fell in love with him cause he was smart."

"Oh! the truth is coming out."

"I feel you are sweet and brave but he can slay any dragon also you are smart enough to know that I'm smater still dont mind that."

"I love that."

"You will be a best dad" by this time I had tears too.

"This is not how I imagined this ending. Us ending."

"Don't be too serious it doesn't suit you. Good night" my heart broke too.

I had two options in front of me. One an ideal behaviour boy ajit,so warm and tight. Second the boy so good I can't even imagine. I could have taken time to answer Ajit. But I know I cannot take second thought of Abhimanyu. I thought for a while and slept for long in sofa.

Dil pe pathar rakhke choose karna pada.

4

It's you

———♡———

"I've always believed in The One, someone. That there's someone out there for me. A perfect match of love calculator, we used to play online when we were small, if you don't know take flame instead. Ok sorry a soulmate. And for The One, I would do anything and everything one can not even imagine wheather it is life or death. I've had my heart broken more than once,(the boyfriend I mentioned actually hurted me that was the first real life relationship i entered.) And things haven't always been easy in my life, I always had real family issues. But all that felt worth it when I met Abhimanyu Jain. I love you. I embrace all of you, even the hard parts (But I was wrong.. about him but by then, it was too late). Really, really, truly." I proposed Abhimanyu. That even make up for the trip fight we had. Out of ego which he hung the call I didn't call back too.He said yes and we went back to our country to marry each other. I was on cloud 9. Left my dreams, moved at his for peace.

We went to my extra rich brother of has a weed farm to solve the problem for us. He belonged to different religion, Abhi. My brother had this huge house and heavy security when we went in the floor shined like diamond. It actually hurted my eyes. He even has a girl as a friend who owns an island of robbed money. We asked my brother to makeup our parents mind for our marriage he suggested to not bother them. Go ahead and marry without them. It hardly matters to him.

Abhimanyu decided to call our parents here in chicago. As they are normal people who don' know much english. Their disability will lead them to connect with each other.

My mom called me as soon as she reaches my apartment " We were told you'll be with us."

"Don't be shy mom. Talk to them they are nice. They won't bite." I replied.

So my mom started a conversation

"If we would have a grand child at least our white picket purgatory would feel logical." my mom said to his mom

" They don't have to move anywhere for schools too. Afterall chicago is the best"his mom replied

"But here are are miles of nosy neighbors, peering suspiciously from behind lawn care equipment and video doorbells."

"But, hey, safest neighborhoodin the state. And who wouldn't sell their soul for that?"

"They , our children have everything so the baby also gets to have everthing."

I heard their this coversation of one random day and came from behind. I added " The perfect family, funded by our parents blood money." and everyone laughed.

We wanted to get here all on our own. You compromise when you have to, when its for them.

They were shocked initially but then agreed to our marriage.We left them alone. Results were great. Our parents became really good friends. And everything was fine. We were of not same religion but only Indians in chicago worked and they started trusting each other. What could go wrong.

And then I realized who I really need to protect. Us. For you, I moved to some soulless, wealthy suburb outside chicago. For peace, I'd marry the cute monster. But there's one part of the old me I can't quite shake. I still beleive in The One. That the right person is out there for me.

I never thought to wonder what happens after boy gets girl. 'Cause we know: And they lived happily ever after.' Fade to black, roll credits. I should have asked more questions. 'Cause I've been in some harrowing situations in my life. But this? I could really use a map.' But I've forged my way in the dark before, I can do it now. I have to. To protect us. I am fucked up and so is he.

Just like essay by Nicholson Baker.Tiny moments made magnificient. Our cards were printed with same warm I don't know why. I was thinking this.

And Abhi came from behind and said "Did you wanted it like a novel by Louisa May Alcott. Hardwork but rewarding. Noble even."

I laughed.

Day one of wedding ceremony where I introduced him and vice versa. we were standing in group.

"So what's the president's name?" shruti asked, teasing me.

"Abhimanyu " I said with a smile.

"So what brings you in?" his friend asked.

"So we had a fight."

" Obviously. You wouldn't be here if you hadn't."

He whispered to me "why are you telling them plus you didn't told me boys were there in the trip"

"I am just having fun" I smiled.

"Good, we're diving right in!"

"It's okay, I won't let anything happen to your image, I promise."

Ajit came in. At a side, says to shruti "The difference is that I almost did a bad thing and she did a terrible thing marrying him. I can't say on what she is doing, so I'm the villain."

"Don't fight, don't make it worse. There's no telling how she'll react." shruti replied

" It's just, sometimes, I get passionate."

"Don't hold your past feelings against yourself." she said with a sigh.

5

We did it to ourselves

A child is being not from birth to a certain limit, in terms of age. And at a certain age, the child is grown and puts away toys and cute behavior. Childhood will come back into our lives, at every stage. No wonder now it's an age to marry.

My card was simple as it said

Shaya Pandit

AND

Abhimanyu Jain

TOGETHER WITH THEIR FAMILIES

REQUEST THE HONOR OF YOR PRESENCE

AT THE CELEBRATION OF THEIR MARRIAGE

SATURDAY, THE THIRTEENTH OF AUGUST

TWO THOUSAND AND TWENTY-ONE

FIVE O'CLOCK IN THE EVENING

421 WOODCRAFT AVE

FORKS

"It's happening." said my mom wave wing the card. She was very happy much more than I am. Some guests were about to come just to eat others for the tradition to give so to get.

I was trying heels for the very first time for my wedding with shruti.

"Try it. You just have to be super confident and you'll nail it, my tomboy," said Shruti

"I've been trying to nail them in. For straight three days. Can I just go barefoot or maybe white bellies?" I replied

"No, absolutely not."

" Just thinking it's a little much more than I would be expected to form Abhi, you know? The dress and the shoes... and all of this. (the decoration)"

"No, it's exactly enough. Tomorrow will be perfect."

"Where do you want them, boss?" asked a tarik a mutual friend of ours to shruti. He was helping workers place the woods.

"On either side of the aisle,"shruti replied

" What aisle?" said some worker carrying woods with him

"Does no one have a vision?" screamed and left. Before leaving she said

"You, go home and get lots of beauty sleep. That's an order"sarcastically

"Ok."

We hugged, I went, she took care of my heels.

I went to meet Abhimanyu

"It's never too late to change your mind," said Abhimanyu

"What? Now you're having second thoughts about me? You are."

"No, I've been waiting my whole life to marry you, Miss." coming towards me to hug me.

"But?" as I pushed him a little away.

"I haven't told you everything about myself. You don't know something. I guess you are supposed to"

"What? You're not a virgin?" We smiled and laughed

"Look, don't scare me away now."

He just had some family issues. Uske ghar pe sirf TV bolta hai.

"Why are you telling me this tonight? Did you think this was going to change my mind about you?"

"I just wondered if it would change your mind about yourself... and who you want to see when you look in the mirror a year from now."

"I know I can do this. Let me tell you why. Because you did. You should give yourself some credit for that. (Grown-up in such environment of parents). Now, hopefully, a year from now... I am going to look in the mirror and see someone like you. I mean, someone capable of courage and sacrifice and love."

Before I could complete

"Come on! Let's go!" his friend shouted

"What is that?" I asked

"I am late for my bachelor party," he said

"Send him out, Shnaya, or we're coming in after him." one of his friends said

"So this party. Will there be strippers?"

"No"

"Don't worry, Shnaya, we'll give him back in plenty of time." again his friend

"Ok, go."

"I'll meet you at the altar."

"I'll be the one in red."

"That was very convincing."

Next day

"What did I say about beauty sleep?" shruti says while doing my makeup for the most special day in any girl's life.

"Sorry, bad dream. It was wedding jitters." I replied

"Do you need some help? I could do her hair." my sister said.

"Really?" I said

"Please," she replied

"Weddings. They bring everyone together." Shruti replied.

"Hey, so, did you find our daughter?" I heard my mom in hallway to dad.

"In here, Mom" I shouted.

My makeup and hair were done as she came in. I was in a bathrobe.

"Oh, my God! You're so beautiful. Oh honey." she was me and started to cry.

"Mom" I laughed

My sister handed her a napkin, she said "Thanks" to her.

My mom called my dad "Get in here"

"You sure? I don't want to..." my dad showing decency

I was shocked he was all suited up.

"I know. I look hot." says my dad

"We thought you needed something blue. And something old" says my mom giving me a gift which she opened the box. It had a gold finished juda pin with zircons.

"It was Grandmother's. But we added the sapphires."

"It's beautiful, you guys. Wow. Thankyou so much." I said hugging them.

"It's your first family heirloom. Pass on to your daughter, and her daughter."my mom said while my sister put it on my bun.

"Mom, I love it." I said and went to hug her as she was crying again but on midway Shruti stopped me.

"Nope. No smudging my masterpiece."

"She is right." my mom said.

"Thankyou" I said to Dad.

"Ok. It's time for the dress." Shruti says showing the dress out of the box.

The stage was set. All decorated with white flowers. Everyone was talking, enjoying the party and talking to each other. I was about to go all dressed up. I saw out for once and got nervous.

"You ready?" my sister asked me.

"Yeah"

Everyone noticed me and stood up.

"Just don't let me fall, girls." I said

"Never" Shruti replied.

I started to walk on a rose petal way. I was anxious by the time him I fell in love. He was wearing this beautiful suit. He looked at me with love in his eyes, happily. He took my hand and I was so happy.

With each pheras there were vow of his and mine.

I Abhimanyu jain, take you Shnaya

To have and to hold.

For better or for worse.

For richer, for poorer.

In sickness and in health.

To love.

To cherish.

As long as we both shall live.

I do

I do.

I love you.

I love you.

I was a child till morning and now I am a wife. For a moment everyone present there vanished for us. Everyone clapped and I literally laughed. Then came the after party or what we say the reception had this huge cake.

"Just thought it'd be bigger" my college friends chatted about the cake.

"Yeah" said another

"hi" Shruti entered into their conversation.

"Hey!"they greeted too."We were just saying how pretty everything is, you know, just saying."

"Well, thanks so much. You don't think it's too much?"

"No"

"Not at all"

I entered as I found something was weird.

"I am happy for both of you." said my friend

"Good to see you." I replied

"Thankyou"

"I hope you'll be happy. We were just trying to appreciate your last night here..."said another. I smiled.

"Look it's not my last night."

"Why did Ajit didn't come?" I asked shruti.

"He though wishes best for you. Don't start something you cannot finish. He not a concern anymore. By the way they are selling pretty fancy champange here." shruti said.

It all went well. He even gave a speech for me. I knew I got to marry this beautiful boy who's nature is so pure. All the glitter in him is gold. Shruti says you guys are star struck lovers, maybe I am the lover and he is the star. It's never too late to say sorry to him for me. I have realised the price of love is a whole damn human being with his tantaurms. I would admit this was not a marriage of convenience we have to make our parents meet. I feel like we are couple of something old and something new. What if he ever had an royal affair, full of pride and bridezilla.

The auspicious day of my marriage was this. We celebrated. My friends and I. Yes, it's true. I've found my love, my soulmate, my sweetheart and I'm receiving greetings for that. My love even brought me the palanquin. The entrance courtyard was decorated to mark this memorable day. My love, your love is my raison d'etre, you are my destiny and I live only through you.

Plus I will not leave my home without the enchanting music of shehnai and the ecststic poems. Listen to me oh cruel one. I had a sumptuous tent set up and of course I brought the palanquin and with fireworks took him along me.

They say marriages are heaven made prayers, we worship. But on the ground, the reality is slightly different. Here, your inner spirit takes a back seat to your address. The sacred union of two souls is what they add. Everyone there was of the beleif that this match is not meant to be. Especially our relatives. They came in heavy embroidered dresses. I wonder why? And even as Me and Abhi circle the sacred fire, all one can hear is... "did he marrying her for love?" or "did he marrying her for the money?". All they can see is that an outsider has clawed his way into the inside. They smile at me.. but only time will tell if he gets accepted. Until then welcome to happy married life.

6

Sorry it had to come to this.

"Every thing is packed and ready to go. Shnaya take my car."Abhi said while I was looking at the mirror.

"I gave you the recorder, right"

"Uh! Yes"

"And you have all the questions"

"Yes"

"You know where you are going."

"I do have a GPS. I can figure it out."

"You are wearing that?" he starred at me with confusions

"Okay maybe a little less talking more eating." I cheacked my self for once and then replied showing him his breakfast.

"Okay bye "

I went interveiw to his office for a new job. I went wearing a saree. His boss was impressed by the indian culture and values. I got the job, I was super excited to tell him but he wasn't happy with the news.

He was rather unhappy and instead of said"Good for you ".

He think I'm getting the job because my family has a famous coffee company. So all Questions he prepared for me was rubbish just about my family. Instaed the people over there were really nice to talk just about me and myself. He got the job by hardwork and I am getting it by my parents name. So I came back from the interview.

"Should I bring a drink."he said

"Yes, please"

"Won't you ask me me how was the interview?" I asked Abhimanyu

"It must be fine" he sayed while sitting and with zero enthusiasm.

"Fine, Just fine"

"They must be really polite and they would have been courteist and very formal and clean"

"Clean"

"Yeah that I remember was my first thought of my interview long back... You wouldn't get it for you I say... They were smart and intense... kind of intimidating."

Though I got pissed of by one line but was interesting to know his feelings or just an interview.

He went on like "I can understand hasination."

"Ah! ha.." I smiled with a look of understanding.

"Why are you looking me like that?" he smiled

"Like what?" I said with a gracious expression.

"Okay I want to make a sandwich. Do you want some?" He got nervous but then gain back his confidence.

"No thanks but you have to admit the interview must have gone ridiculously lit."

"I'm sure if you get attracted to that sort of that sort of scenarios"

"The nervous feelings"

"They didn't make me nervous."

"Now you're defending them."

"Let's keep our private life personal. They are few things in my office that require my touch. You enjoyed today? hope to see you tomorrow." he said and left.

The Interveiw page said: (I read on the way)

Shnaya Pandit interveiw

New building,

3rd Ave, Seattle, WA

May, 5, 2.00 PM

Special Graduation edition

Questions:

You are very young to amassed such an empire. To what do you owe your success to?

I mummbled the answer I write, work at my parents bussiness and invest in stocks.

Many successful enterperneurs and bussiness people have a guidline philosphy.Do your parents have some? If so what?

Your brother make huge investment in the manufacturing in United states- Not only in seattle but also Detroit. Other companies are re-locating their manufacturing division to Far east and in developing countries, why do he continue to invest in US.?

And other few rubbish question

I miss when he used to look at me, like we were ever in love.

Just like every other marriage, our marrige was going well till Day1,2, maybe3 but surely not 4. We went on a honeymoon when it started. In maldives, any random resort

"This place is so beautiful. Its surreal to have a honeymoon." I said

"There's nothing new about this" he sighed

I found that a bit weird, he showed no interest.

"By the way we meet on this crossroad right?"

"You gotta keep me focused, no one knows whether we'll ever come here again. So stay for a moment right here."

He lands to bed and says "the creases of these soft sheets are calling you right now "don't go away" they say Where else is such comfort?"

"My heart knows but look at the sky its so different right now my heart doesn't agree to sleep."

"Just like the running engines of a car your heart is restless."

"So, what, we must part?"

He smiled.

"Smile for me once more"

He putted a pillow on his face.

The door bell rang and there was this concert pamphlet. He started doing his laptop.

"Do you wanna go to this concert?"

He didn't even notice me.

"So tell me, talk to me now."

He went to the next little room we had, putting on his headphone. I got annoyed. The very next day I left that hotel went to my chicago house. If he has a soft heart. Every little things happened to him mattered then why not me. I going to make him feel the same, I decided. He used to cry in order to get me, where was the love now.

I was upset in my home when he called "I know you don't want to talk to me but just a reminder the empty house of yours have curtains of white colour which may flow in wind also the clock make a sharp tick tick with a pause sound which may scare you, but don't get scared for I'm right here with you."

It was his way to say I love you. I said "Sorry I should have given you a second chance."

"I anyway had work."

"Does it even feel to you, these things"

"Sometimes yes, right moments makes the worth."

"By the way I have to buy a vase. A vase broke in anger, you took time to call."

"It takes time to process things. That vase was priceless."

"It was cheap and tacky"

"It can't be undo."

"Okay I broke a vase."

Like these we had enumors number of fight. No the small once but of cheating. To help our relationship we even went to pshycologist. She was nice, tricks and tips didn't work. I became psyche. The fights were this loud and mad. Screaming and crying was what our neighbours could get for the gossip. He used to say to me to speak quietly.

But he used to come back each time he used to leave. Things went teary apart. I tore his clothes once. We never celebrated birthday together we didn't even celebrated it. He twice said it's over on my face. Was the marrige worth the pain. But the worst was yet to come. He used to try to explain things, calm me down but when I used to push him away (emotionally and physically both) he used to start blaming me too.

I once even scratched his face(whole damn cheek) it did bleeded and went to my office mascara spread all over my eyes. I was insane. I used to be jealous too. Once out of jealously I threw a vase of flower on his face hard. Thank god he was saved he bend down. Maybe it wasn't meant to be for forever. I cry now too. I even threw his new phone in the fountain. Tore his potrait which I made.

Burned his clothes and thew them out my balcony too. Love's a torture anyway. We should have told to each other, said to each other. Now we can't say no one warned us. He was no less too, ate a juicy mango, crushed it in the mouth and splitted it on my face.

Okay I was worse I took a golf stick and hitted the bonnet of his car, he just bought. The reason was we had many memories in it. He came to stop me. I even putted the stick into the logo too. He begged and requested me several times to stop. Eventually he had to leave the town in an broken car.

I was madly in love with him at some point of my life, the world knows, but he still doesn't love me at all. . . I am not sure what type of intoxication he consumes and he becomes so ignorant. To update you about now the days of him complaining in secret are gone now he look straight into my eyes and shout argue about notted points about us.

In private sector when we work our personality is what showed to others to attract. It's a part of work we do. When I used to go for high proffessional meeting for eg to meet celebrity me and my companions are given top branded clothes for photo comes in magizine of the deal. The stylist started giving me black to wear. Maybe that became my personality.

It became difficult for me to breathe and when I tried to clear the environment and one day told him "It's really hard to breathe him I want to leave." He said "Get a famous tatto of breathe too while leaving."

Our marriage was on the verge to be broken but somewhere family, somewhere past memories, and what will our neighbours think kept us in a cage, where we became loins for each other. It became jungle for us or we became the junglees. Shanaya sometimes beleived he had an affair, checked his phone and all.

Kabhi kabhi lagta hai wo MBA se mummy jo bolri thi usse shaadi karleti toh zyada aacha tha. Hum actually special log se zyada expect karlete hain unhe close ni lana chaiye.

7

Its been a long time since we fell in love.

⎯⎯⎯⎯♡⎯⎯⎯⎯

I came to India again to extend my passport. So my sister opened a new clinic. Out of the stress I had all these fight, I skiped on my days. I went for a normal checkup. Me and my mom enjoyed the inaguration party. She takes me with her where ever she goes.

The reports came on hand I opened the envelope she said "suffering from preeclampsia."

I stood up with shakky hands. Got an horrified look from mom. Both the main doctor and my sister stared at me. I have to be uncomfortable throughout the gestational period of my pregnancy. Its a disease.

I went out to a safe place to cry. It was worse then a breakup. Losing a part of body. I wonder where was my mistake in this. Did I ever heart someone so that god gave me this.

Kafi baar hota hai khushi mein words ni hote bayan karne ke liye iss pehli baar dukh mein ni the.

I thought for a while. Why is God going off about something I said, maybe he doesn't my humour like

Abhimanyu do. It was such a typical day and look what I got to hear. Something no one would like. No one knows my story like I do.

But a thought like a dream just struck me. I just woke up today found that the reason we were fighting for was here, the whole time. I called Abhimanyu.

"I have called you for a reason today. You know I'm not going to continue with our relationship. Maybe I am not the water you need to satify your thirst. (I first tried to end with the topic fight but don't know how he got to know. Lter I discovered he has putten a microscope in my mobile as he wanted to keep a check that I don't hurt my self in aggression. Even in the tough times he held me.) It's over I want a divorce."

"You think I've burned the cover of shame. I am not this shallow. I am not leaving you alone in such a moment alone. All the blame is on me and promise it would never happen again. Don't you dare to say I deserve better."he replied.

I smiled at him.

"There are other options we can try."

"We can adaopt. Lets adopt now. I was anyway coming to talk to our parents about the anger issue.I will come now to adopt noow just intwo day. By then take care. Should I hold the call?"

"No I'm fine."

"Yes you are much stronger then what I think."

"You too."

People have been trying to explain my madness to him. He still kept loving me and adoring me. Two days later when he came. I went to airport. The colour of my eyelids were not kohl, it's blood. If we would have told this to someone, they wouldn't have respected us.

We never fought since then. At that time he once said "I've been here all along, you didn't saw me?"`

"I can see you are the one who understands me."

We adopted a brown baby girl who has a smile that can light up whole world. The nun there said she hasn't seen a this smile before. She said she was fine but I know her better than that.

Once you get a child, it felt better. Food seemed worth.

I even know what makes her laugh when she is about to cry. I know her favorite songs and she tells me about her dream.

To Abhi her hair hair is lovely, he is allergic.

He reads novels to her, takes her to library.

Plays with her. His all office know her. Parenting is fun and a difficult job too.

She once vomited on her novel. Pee on his face. Laugh out loud. He is considerate. We are both good for each other but sometimes I wonder did God think bad for a child. But he has blessed us now. We take care of her now. She is happy of new family. My mom is happy for me. Me and Abhi never fought after that. Every thing was going well but..

We wanted to enjoy every monent of our live with her. She is this precious. She is cute and have lovely dominating nature. Shnaya wonders one day her daughter we learn reading and will read this too. Growing up with kids is surreal. I every day bring toys for her. I was enthusiastic about shoping but there is no new stuff we have brought for us after she has come home. We have started laughing together, all of us.

Our relationship healed. We started seeing thing much more clear. He gazed at me in sunshine asked me to "Come and hold my hand"

I felt his hand and held his wrist. I can see a new me, after past those days. I didn't elaborated much because I was told not to go back to hard times. It leads to depression and I surely not my readers want to cry. No its not my story its fiction and good for mental health.

Abhimanyu held shnaya's cheek "We are mortal"he said. We look at mirror together. He said "You are strong." After the hug he continued.

"Our daughter, she is increadible"

"I have to see her" I as I wanted to go towards her but he held me back

"Wait. wait. Lets have a drink first."

"Amazed. You brought me here, talked to me. Even mature people have problem in that."

He cried and added "You're still here."

"So are you."

"didn't expect to see you seem so new."

"So creep to be honest..."

"I would keep my distance for now, I'll have a check on our daughter "

"Safer for baby future if you do me first"

"Since when do you care so much."

"We really look good together." as he says he leaves.

"Such a sparkly environment you created it's great"

"I was seeing our wedding video. Do you wanna have look, I bring our daughter here" as he switched onn the TV

"She lives in peace with us."

"Oh what's a wedding without some family drama." he said

The video started

It was speeches of everyone.

It had lines like Shnaya was like everyone else mesmerized by Abhimanyu or his hair since school days, shruti said.

I would like to thank shnaya's parents for bringing such a wonderful person into the world. We will cherish an protect her forever, says my mother in law.

"It's an extraordinary thing to meet someone whom you can bear your soul to. Who accept you for what you are. I was waiting since for a very long time to get beyond of who I am. With Shnaya I feel like I can finally begin. My beautiful beautiful wife, no measure of time will be long enough. We'll start with forever."

Everyone cheered and I was in tears.

There was video of dance of my parents, there were twirls and rolls.

"That was so kind of you" I said as it ended.

"Kind is one another name."

He putted our daughter to sleep and then hugged and lifted me up with a twirl as the song played behind.

"Where have you been?" I said

"Why? Are you okay!"

"I am here."

Cell phone beeps.

"Its time to say goodbye." says Abhimanyu.

"It's fine."

Before going "You know I'll always going to be home."

"I love you, always am and always will."

We just paused for moment and starred at each other. He smile as though he is an idot. I didn't because I know he's not.

Days later we were going on a road trip.

My mom called "Can you tell me where is taking you."

"It's a suprise to me."

She cheered us and she happy about our relationship.

Budhape mei unko tension de deya tha meine bhi jhagde karke. Waise hote choti choti baat the. like one for example was I once started questioning my marriage I thought Ajit ke sath kahin nashe me padi hoti wo zyada better. He got offended on that and it continued...

Dad ne to bhagwan ke hath pair jod liye the. Sab dusre religion wale ladke se shaadi karli thi na uspe jaara tha.

Kya aur time lena tha usse samjhne mei phir shaadi kari thi, ek min shaadi toh karni he ni thi bilkul bhi isse, aage badhne ke pehleaur time spend karna tha?.. Wo kehta hai tum ghar pe reh reh ke frustate ho jati ho isiliye.. kya pata aap log darne ki zaroorat ni hai first mein fictional hoon, second mein itti guusa wali ni hoon shruti se puchlena oh sorry wo bhi fiction hai. Ek aur baat abh mein ni karne wali wo sab bechare pe even if aapko maza aaya uss drame me.

8

Push the limits of love

Things went well after the adaoption. So here was the road trip.

I was nervous We hired a caretaker for our daughter, we haven't named her yet. It's my sister in laws duty in our religion to name the child. Abhimanyu wanted us to name her in india with all the ritual and friends and family. Even shruti has't met her yet. Should I name her shruti. LOL.

The music played in our car soft and sweet tone. It was getting night I could hear dogs bark aloud at night out of cold. Wonder why doesn't government make street dogs wear sweater. The reflection on the glass of the door showed my face on which the trees were movig behind as we went forward.

The master pieces, statues on the mid way were all lighten up. We took a taxi, outstation he hugged in the back seat of a prime sedan. I saw people dancing and drum playing on some islamic song. He held my hand in a way fingers across fingers. People cheering and partying were all around.

He took me to the dance floor where the whole city was dancing on that street. I got dtruck to the waiter too. We just came close and danced a bit, just for name sake. We just wanted to enjoy. we then took a boat.

"So we are not staying here." I asked

"No" he replied while putting the bags in the boat. I was super excited, I couldn't stop smiling.

"Any clues!" I asked. He just smiled.

The boat was literally jumping on water. We hooted. At night, there was not one in the else then us in water which was also a matter of concern but we didn't. If we would've then whats love. We reached an island where I saw a huge vineyard poster, taller than me. I went in, saw my brother there. I got excited alot because he never comes to our place.

"Your brother helped me buying it. It's for our daughter. She'll learn about grapes and all."

I was amused to see my family cooperation towards him. He planned this from the begining, the very first day he met my brother. But we're parents we generally give it on the name our child. I know he loved me from way back them.

"It's perfect for her."

"Before bringing her here I wanted you to have a look and plan the decoration and all for her."

"I love it as it is. Simple as our family."

"Sure? Do you wanna have a drink?"

"Yeah, it's a celebration."

"Before you drink. The people here are religious to have to get a checkup done."

"Oh okay"

Moments later a report came that said I cannot drink wine. I am pregnant with twins. I asked hyhem to recheck but they were right. The previous report had some error.

I was happy and on top of the world. We got chance to be parents again. He actually saw me for the first time with love in his eyes.

9

After party

———◆♡◆———

We went back India where Abhimanyu bought a fort as our house. My three children grew there.

My children grew fastest. Today they were born and tomorrow passed their college. My elder daughter is a star, tara rightly named.

Tarun and Varun are exacty opposite. Varun's our heart. Love and respect us alot. With tarun there comes a story. He was rude and angry to all.

When we used ask him generally "How was your day?"

"Agar aacha ni bhi hua hoga toh aapse kya matlab?"

we got him married to a birdie, cute little girlwho spended time with him. One day she was gone sick and that time varun realised he actually loves her. She completely changed him. He became a gentleman. Cute, right?

Being a mom to them was like having 3 more friends to the party.

Akhir kitna kuch dekha inn bachoon ka meine hasna rona gana.

My very new bride has a past history too.

10

They didn't make things worth I'll spend my money to.

───────── ♡ ─────────

After moving to India, I had nothing to do again. After kids it's difficult to manage family and children both and coming from such mental state it's ridiculously impossible. I can get exhausted which will lead to anger issuess again.

I was this beautiful boy in ane of the other sister I have of my dad's side, he was of 2years age. He used to only eat salads from others plate.

I suggested same for kiki she was thin too. but her parents got upset. My sister got offended because I indirectly said her child is thin.

I didn't go to work as my children were small So I started to write with zero pressure. I wrote about motherhood and how manage life after babies. He still teased me to write about how to spend parents money. One day he said he is serious write about this topic and no one has thought about it. About how to spend money and not waste it. I can't beleive him sometimes.

He secreatly left his job and started studing for upsc for me as i wanted to be in civil services. He could only have 2years for preparation he cannot risk more than that his job as our savings ended. He enjoyed the process of learning he failed the exam but my dreams were successfull the day i realised he was studing for me.

The book I wrote was published in a free platform which gained a lot of success. It became bestseller and I can't be more proud of that. We stopped taking money from our parent which i started when we first adopted.

Before I'll tell my after fame story. There was this one incident close to my heart.

Our adopted daughter, there is no shame to be adopted, was brought in sad condition of the family. We all healed with her smile and there is no doubt we are happy cause of only her. I can also say it children help a marriage work too but primarily it depends on us.

We actually went through pain of pregnancy, my traumas, and not even know what else will also include. She was all the time with us 100% cooperative. But I felt she could understand too that we were ignoring her, maybe it was our failure. We spended more time with our twin kids and invested more on them, it happened naturally.

One day I went to her and told my strong girl the reality for is she becomes mature she wouldn't be insecure.

"Mein tumhari maa ni hoon, na hi tum mer beti ho, humara by blood koi relation ni hai but dil se hai. Mein tumhari maa banne ki koshish bhi ni karri kyunki jhooti ma ke sath khelne mein tumhe maza ni aayega . Mein jaan mujhke khush hoeigi to tumhe samaj mein aayega. Tum meri beti banne ki galti bhi mat karna jaisi ho waisi he rehna mujhe tum pasand ho. Mein sirf tumhari dekbhal karna chahti hoon. Jitna mein kar sakti hoon. Tum mujhe maa he bulana apne bhaiyon ki tarah. Aur mein humesha hoon tumhare liye."

When I told him he said you shouldn't have done this, you made her mature before her age, she would have understand it with time. Maybe if not she would have said something to us on her own. It was a task and you literally gave up. How happily she would have lived with us if we are her own parent her tantrums would be beared by us.

"What if she never said anything to us and beared a pain for long time. We have not yet put her b'day date yet. What if she grows into someone who doesn't like her parents."

"We'll celebrate her b'day with other kids."

The book she wrote became successful, when the children were small she met a new coming singer who suggested a plan to date for her family didn't came in fame. Just for the promotion of books and songs he wrote. Dating gets famous on hand. She agreed to it. But once the paprazi people saw Shnaya with her small daughter tara. Shnaya thought now the news will come ot and the media will accept the happy family it's supposed to be. But it went wrong the news asumed tara as the singers child. They had two option 1 to gain fame of the child, 2 to tell the truth. If they hid the truth the only thing would be children have to remember their cousins name. But they choose to tell the truth and both happy family was happily accepted. They didn't wanted the children to suffer even a bit.

11

The fort we live in

❦

The fort we live in came with a story of itself. Ni aisi koi daravni story ni warna hum ni lete ye fort.

There was this huge kingdom the king owned. Jo abh humara ghar hai. Kya karuin Abhi ne kharida ne kharida hai bola foreign sabhyayta mein bohot reh chuke abh indian ki bari.

Haa.. aur 3 bacho ka personal private space bhi banate banate itna kharcha aur bada ban he jata.

The king of the kingdom always wore dark green clothes of heavy embroiderey, shoes of gold not glitter and had hair till shoulder. He used to wash his hair regularly and super neat and clean. He had silky soft hair and was praised by his parents and he was too a devotee to his parents. He was supposed to be dark character but became a good one.

Do aache logo mein choose karna diificult hai. Mein bhi ni choose kar payi thi Ajit and abhimanyu mein. Bas situation jaisi banti hain hum waise chale jatein hain.

The king married to a beautiful queen who was traeted like a one and not like his wife. She used to dressup with friends in a dance and song. They became the best example of supposed to be.

But with time the queen became sad out of loneliness that was the time Our queen found her soulmate. A sepoy of the empire who criticized king for his heavy tax thats when the queen defended the king. The sepoy then went to queen with flowers to apologize and slowly queen conved her other feeling they fell in love, she then elopes with the sepoy and lives happily ever after.

Epilogue

So this was Shnaya and her chosen family. To be honest, being a mom and writting love story of my own kid is bit weird.

Mere bete varun ko bhi aisi ladki se pyaar hua tha jo bohot sundar thi. I mean hai. Usne mujhse ek baar pucha tha.

"Mom agar usne mere flaws dekhliye to shaadi ke baad pure time toh properly nahi reh sakta"

"Darro mat uske bhi flaws hoeinge." I can relate to him i was this nervous too.

We lived our happily ever after.